I am a GORILLA

Steve Macleod

Go to www.av2books.com, and enter this book's unique code.

BOOK CODE

Z992834

AV² by Weigl brings you media enhanced books that support active learning.

AV² provides enriched content that supplements and complements this book. Weigl's AV² books strive to create inspired learning and engage young minds in a total learning experience.

Your AV² Media Enhanced books come alive with...

Audio
Listen to sections of the book read aloud.

Video
Watch informative video clips.

Embedded Weblinks
Gain additional information for research.

Try This!
Complete activities and hands-on experiments.

Key Words
Study vocabulary, and complete a matching word activity.

Quizzes
Test your knowledge.

Slide Show
View images and captions, and prepare a presentation.

... and much, much more!

Published by AV² by Weigl
350 5th Avenue, 59th Floor New York, NY 10118
Website: www.av2books.com   www.weigl.com

Macleod, Steve.
Gorilla / Steve Macleod.
    p. cm. -- (I am)
ISBN 978-1-61690-757-0 (hardcover : alk. paper) -- ISBN 978-1-61690-764-8 (softcover : alk. paper)
1. Gorilla--Juvenile literature. I. Title.
 QL737.P96M33 2011
 599.884--dc22

                    2010052409

Printed in the United States of America in North Mankato, Minnesota
1 2 3 4 5 6 7 8 9 0 15 14 13 12 11

052011
WEP37500

Project Coordinator: Aaron Carr Art Director: Terry Paulhus

Weigl acknowledges Getty Images as the primary image supplier for this title.

I AM A GORILLA

In this book, I will teach you about

- myself

- my food

- my home

- my family

and much more!

I am a gorilla.

4

I slap my chest to talk.

6

I use my feet like hands.

8

I walk on my hands and feet.

I am carried
for the first three months
of my life.

I eat more than 100 kinds of plants.

14

I spend seven hours eating every day.

16

I make two new beds every day.

I live in tropical forests.

I am a gorilla.

GORILLA FACTS

This page provides more detail about the interesting facts found in the book. Simply look for the corresponding page number to match the fact.

Pages 4-5

I am a gorilla. Gorillas have short bodies, with thick chests and long arms. On its face, a gorilla has round ears, large nostrils, and a sloping forehead. Most of its body is covered in dark hair. In nature, adult male gorillas can grow to be 6 feet (1.8 meters) tall and weigh more than 500 pounds (227 kilograms).

Pages 6-7

A gorilla slaps its chest to talk. This is often followed by other communication signals, such as running sideways, pulling on plants or grass, and slapping the ground. Like people, gorillas also sneeze, cough, yawn, hiccup, burp, and laugh.

Pages 8-9

Gorillas use their feet like hands. They can do this because their big toe works like a thumb. This helps gorillas pick up and hold onto objects using their feet, just like they do with their hands.

Pages 10-11

Gorillas walk on their hands and feet. It is a special kind of movement called "knuckle-walking." To move like this, gorillas put their feet flat on the ground. Then, they put their weight on the back of their hands and pull their legs forward.

Baby gorillas are carried for the first three months of their lives. After three months, baby gorillas will begin to ride on their mother's back. After three years, gorillas learn to climb trees.

Gorillas eat more than 100 different kinds of plants. A gorilla's main diet is made up of leaves, shoots, and stems. Sometimes, they eat fruit. There is a lot of water in the leaves of the plants gorillas eat, so they do not drink water.

Gorillas spend seven hours eating every day. In that time, a gorilla can eat up to 50 pounds (23 kg) of food. That would be the same as eating 41 loaves of bread.

Gorillas make two new beds every day. These beds are called nests. Gorillas build one nest to rest in during the day and another to sleep in at night. They build their nests on the ground or in trees.

Gorillas live in tropical forests. They also live in swamps and fields, located near the equator in Africa. These nature areas are being developed to make more room for people. Gorillas are now an endangered species. There are fewer than 206,000 gorillas in the world.

WORD LIST

Research has shown that as much as 65 percent of all written material published in English is made up of 300 words. These 300 words cannot be taught using pictures or learned by sounding them out. They must be recognized by sight. This book contains 30 common sight words to help young readers improve their reading fluency and comprehension. This book also teaches young readers several important content words, such as proper nouns. These words are paired with pictures to aid in learning and improve understanding.

Page	Sight Words	Page	Content Words
4	a, am, I	4	gorilla
6	I, my, to	6	chest, slap, talk
8	hand, I, like, my, use	8	feet
10	and, hand, I, my, on, walk	10	feet
12	am, carry, first, for, I, my, of, the, three	12	life, month
14	eat, I, kind, more, of, than	14	plant
16	day, eat, every, I, seven	16	hour, spend
18	day, every, I, make, new, two	18	bed
20	a, am, I, in, live	20	gorilla, tropical, forest

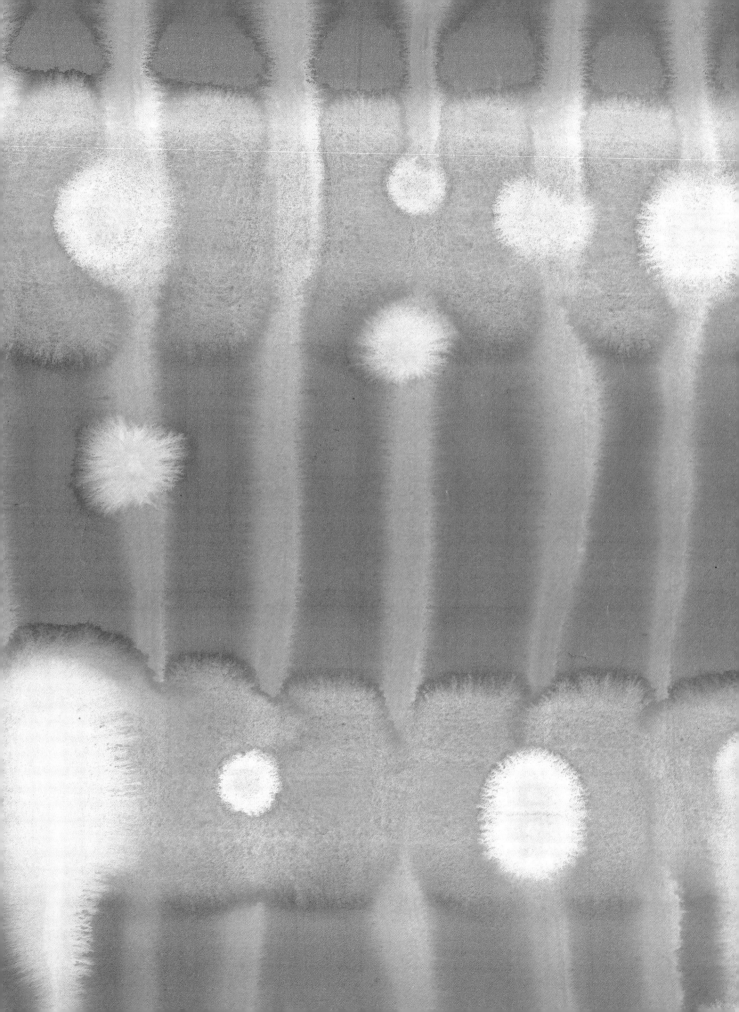

SQUARE
FISH

An Imprint of Macmillan

ANTARCTICA. Copyright © 1990 by Helen Cowcher.
All rights reserved. Printed in October 2009 in Singapore by Tien Wah Press (Pte) Ltd.
For information, address Square Fish, 175 Fifth Avenue, New York, NY 10010.

Square Fish and the Square Fish logo are trademarks of Macmillan and
are used by Farrar, Straus and Giroux under license from Macmillan.

Library of Congress catalog card number: 89-45911
ISBN: 978-0-312-58979-0

Originally published in the United States by Farrar, Straus and Giroux
Square Fish logo designed by Filomena Tuosto
First Square Fish Edition: 2009
10 9 8 7 6 5 4 3 2 1
www.squarefishbooks.com

ANTARCTICA

HELEN COWCHER

SQUARE
FISH

FARRAR, STRAUS AND GIROUX

NEW YORK

In the cold far south, in Antarctica,
live emperor penguins, Weddell seals,
and Adélie penguins.

The emperor penguin lays her egg in winter, when it is dark both day and night. Then she leaves to feed at sea. While she is gone, her mate carefully nestles the egg on top of his feet for two months.

He huddles in a tight circle with his friends, against the freezing winter storms.

Meanwhile, his mate is feeding at sea

. . .where danger lurks.

A ferocious leopard seal!

Luck is with the emperor this time.
She leaves the water safely and trudges
back to the rookery.

There is great excitement because their chick has just hatched.

But the male emperor is hungry and weak. It is his turn to go to sea to find food.

When it is spring, the sun at last
shines again in the Antarctic sky.
A Weddell seal climbs onto the ice
to have her pup.

The Adélie penguins have also come onto the ice. On their long journey to the rocky shore, where they will lay their eggs, they pass the emperor chicks.

The Adélies build their nests out of pebbles. They take turns keeping the eggs warm until the hatching.

Just beyond the nesting place, some
men have built a base camp.

Suddenly the Adélies hear
a terrible whirring noise:
helicopters! They panic and
leave their eggs unguarded.

Skuas swoop in to have a feast!

Frightened by the helicopters, the Adélies will not nest here again.

The emperors, too, are uneasy. They have heard huge explosions, and seen ice and rock hurled high into the air.

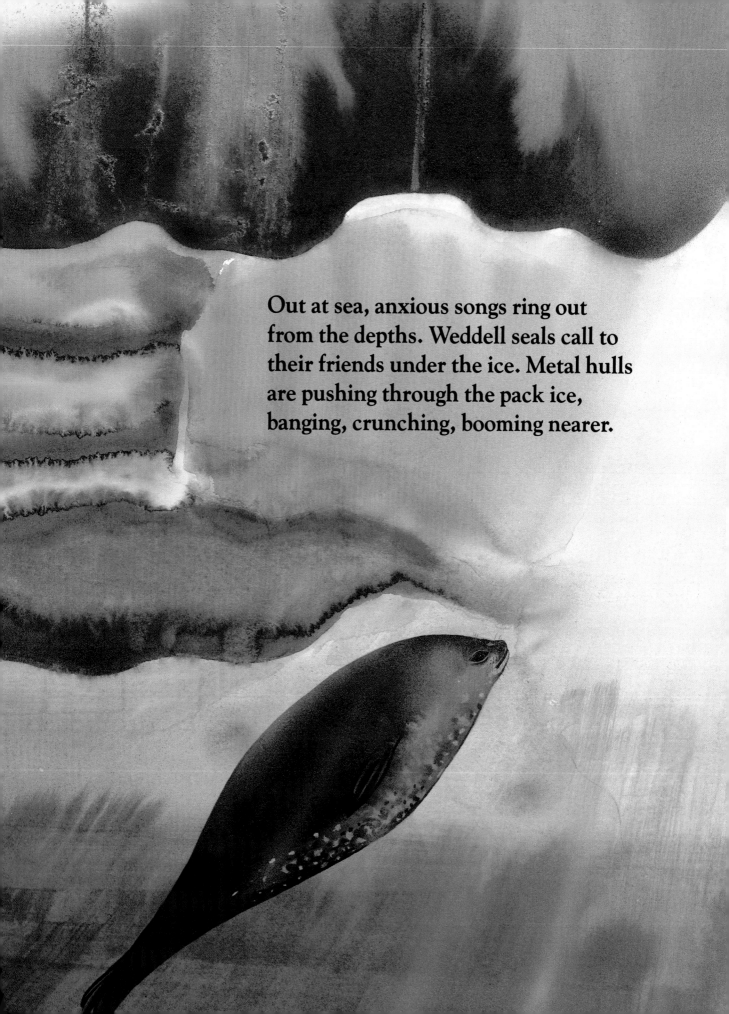

Out at sea, anxious songs ring out from the depths. Weddell seals call to their friends under the ice. Metal hulls are pushing through the pack ice, banging, crunching, booming nearer.

The penguins and the seals have always shared their world with ancient enemies, the skuas and the leopard seals. But these new arrivals are more dangerous. The seals and penguins cannot tell yet whether they will share or destroy their beautiful Antarctica . . .

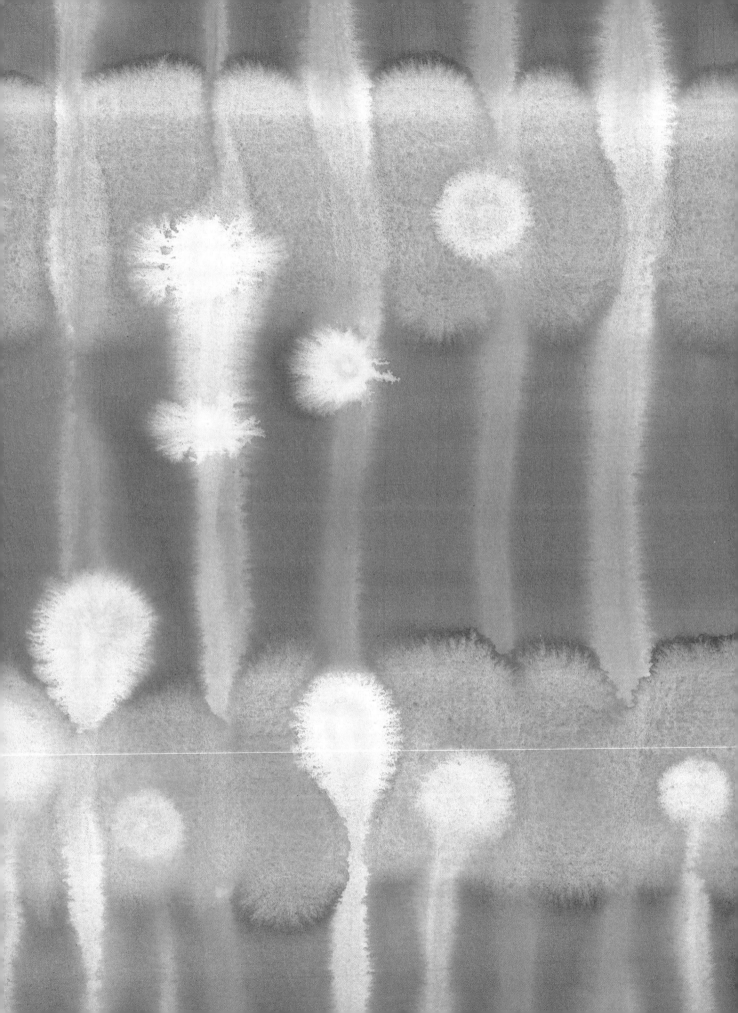

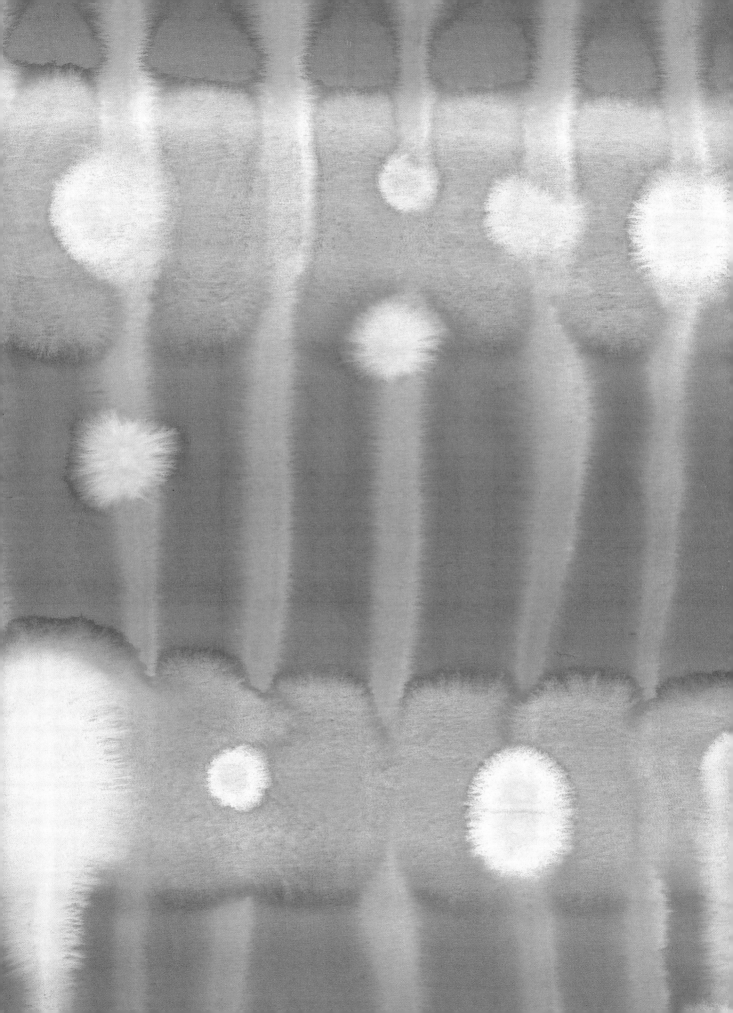